10 Tips for Applying for Government Jobs

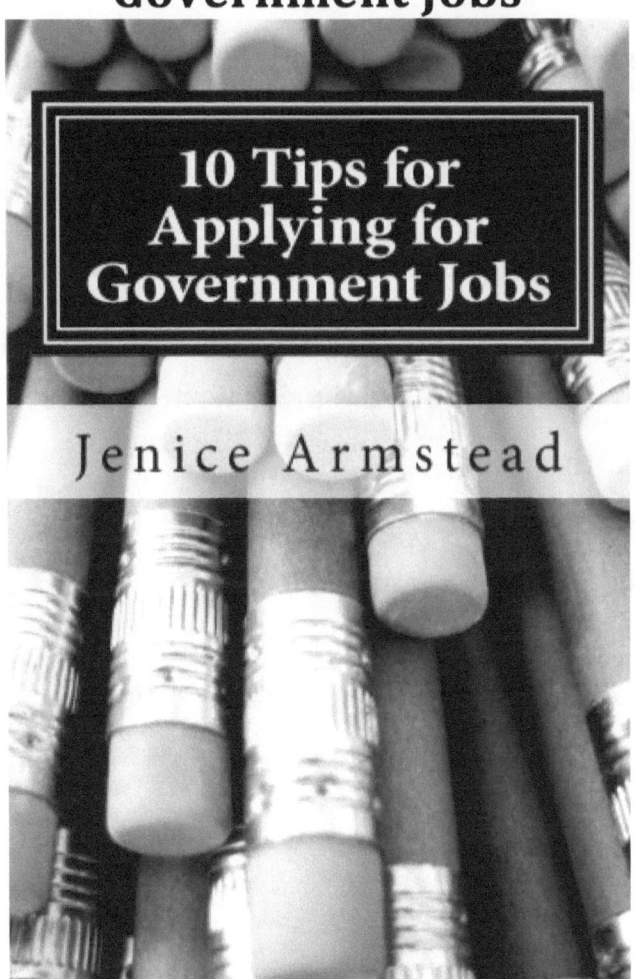

Easy Methods for Job Seekers

10 Tips for Applying for Government Jobs

6" x 9" (15.24 x 22.86 cm)
Black & White on Cream paper
80 pages
ISBN-13: 978-1481901642 (CreateSpace-Assigned)
ISBN-10: 1481901648
BISAC: Business & Economics / Reference

Disclaimer

The reader should use their own judgment in utilizing the information in this book. The reader should seek advice from professionals as needed. The author's advice and information are based on professional experiences The author/publisher shall have neither responsibility nor liability to any person or entity with respect to any damages directly or indirectly as an aspect by any advice or information contained herein.

Dedication

This book and series is dedicated to the job seeker, you are not alone in your career goals. Take all options as opportunities; remember you are the human capital fabric of the economy.

Be empowered,
Dr. Jenice Armstead

Photo Credit: Robert Cass

TABLE OF CONTENTS

Biography

Dr. Jenice Armstead is a military veteran, author, motivational speaker, Professor and Academic Business Department Chair with over 17 years professional experience in the public and private sector. Jenice's expertise covers human resources, business management, the federal hiring process and government hiring policy. She understands the significance of human capital value for organizational development. She has an exceptional aptitude for teaching difficult topics with practical approaches. Jenice has a MBA with a Concentration in Human Resources from Saint Leo University and a Doctorate of Business Administration from Jones International University.

Forward

The job market has changed; it has changed for the better in many ways. This economy has bounced back from one of the worst economic down falls of this century. The job market is flooded with new job seekers and excellent opportunities for the taking. The need for fresh talent is apparent; the need for new ideas is infectious. New graduates, new job seekers and new ways of understanding this new job market are more concentrated than ever before ... these are all apart of the new equations of obtaining employment opportunities for the job seeker.

The federal sector is hiring, let it be clear that the federal sector has created jobs and internships. There are a few things that job seekers must understand about obtaining employment in this federal sector job market. The federal sector is more organized than ever before. The federal sector has gone through a reform of implementing new job hiring practices. The federal sectors new job hiring practices include: the use of extensive interviews, panels of board members, personality tests, demonstration of work knowledge, skills, abilities and job experience.

There are some great ways for job seekers to "stand out" from the competition, but first the job seeker needs to understand the loop holes when it comes to finding and applying for federal employment in this new job market. Do not be discouraged in this new job market. You are the "human capital" fabric of the economy.

This new job market requires the creation and use of multiple resumes, live website links to electronic resumes, and resume social media sites. Job seekers need to keep the information up to date at all times, and most of all a full understanding of what their "digital finger print" looks like. When I say "digital finger print" I mean, understanding what public information is available for potential employers to search and find via the Internet. It is good practice to "Google" or look up oneself up on the Internet to see what information is publicly available for all to view. Just as one would conduct a "Credit Score" clean up, a "digital finger print" is just as important to conduct on a quarterly basis.

Federal government positions are not as difficult to apply for, as most believe they are. Many times there are document requirements, time requirements, and pre-qualifications to read carefully before job seekers can complete the federal government job application. Most federal government job announcements are conducted completely online at www.usajobs.gov. A computer and Internet connection are two initial requirements of the federal hiring process. Job seekers must create a USAJOBs profile to get stared. This may sound like a lot, but in fact once you read this book you will realize that it sounds a lot scarier than it is to complete. The federal sector job hunting experience is all about organization and attention to detail.

You have come to the right place to get your "10 Tips for Applying for Government Jobs." The federal hiring process involves due process, time requirements, deadlines and required documents. One of the main keys is to read the entire job announcement you are applying for. It is a good practice to print the entire job announcement out and use a highlighter to ensure all of the "T's" are crossed and "I's" are dotted.

In the government hiring process, entire applications can be completely removed or "trashed" if the application package is not completed by the candidate, by the deadline. There are no "ifs, ands or butts," hiring managers are not legally required to extend deadlines unless there is a viable reason to do so. In most cases, only disabled applicants have this benefit. In this case, the disabled applicant must provide documentation for the disability to qualify for receiving an application extension.

These are only a few of the topics that are covered in "10 Tips for Applying for Government Jobs." This book was created for the job seeker to keep this book on hand to organize, keep track of and provide a greater understanding of the government hiring process.

This book will start you off in the right direction with providing the job seeker 10 tips for applying for federal government job announcements and positions.

Things You Will Need for Success

There are a few items that will be needed to ensure success during the federal government hiring process:

Physical Items

Computer

Internet Connection

Printer

Pens/Pencils

Printer Paper

Highlighter(s)

Mental Items

Patience

Time & Effort

Motivation

It is vital to remember that success is measured only by the limitations the job seeker puts on himself or herself. In this unconventional job market, the job seeker needs to be extra confident, skilled, and self-assured their career and professional goals are absolutely clear. This means making lists, taking quality time to understand the strengths and weaknesses of their field. The job seeker needs to have the ability to understand the difference between options and opportunities, which may be presented in unlikely ways. This new job market is unlike any other, and opportunities will come in all shapes and forms. An open mind, motivation and keeping current will benefit the job seeker in achieving ultimate success in their field of choice. This is just the beginning of a plethora of opportunities to be presented. Awareness is key. Keeping accurate records of jobs, which have been applied for, will ensure the job seekers organization and tailoring job opportunity endeavors. Keeping a list of positive affirmations will reassure the job seeker in times of doubt and apprehension. Some examples of positive professional affirmations include:

- o I am working toward my goals
- o I am the best candidate for the position
- o I have everything it takes to be successful
- o I have excellent communication skills
- o I am approachable and likeable

These are just a few of the positive affirmations job seekers should have written down in a attainable place for the times when verbal reassurance is needed to keep a positive attitude about the job search progress, interviews, or if only to read aloud when doubt starts to surface. Affirmations are easily accustomed toward any situation the job seeker chooses to use the affirmation for. The goal of affirmations is to reassure, motivate and guide the mind toward the positive spectrum of thinking.

Positive thinking is not enough to get a position, but keeping a positive attitude about the job seeking process will show to benefit how the job seeker feels while going through the process. In this job market, an attitude can make or break a job seekers opportunity. Being positive is not a cliché, it could be a matter of getting a job opportunity or not.

Remember, you can truly do anything you put your mind to with motivation, focus, organization and persistence.

I wish you all the best in following your dreams and goals.

All the Best,

Dr. Jenice Armstead

10 Tips for Applying to Government Jobs Introduction

Today's economy is brutal for the job seeker. Many businesses have conducted massive layoffs, furloughs, forced retirement programs and cut-backs. This is where the federal government has picked up the slack. The federal government has created jobs and is hiring. In contradiction to what you hear in the news or read in the papers, the federal government is growing the economy. With increased opportunities for job seekers looking for work, the federal government has improved hiring practices.

There are tons of internships, temporary, contractor, part-time, full-time and volunteer positions waiting to be filled by the federal government. The federal hiring process is not perfect, but there are ways to increase your chances when applying for these federal positions.

You have come to this book for a number of reasons. Whether it is to gain a better perspective of applying for federal jobs, how to gain knowledge about the federal hiring practices or to simply understand the basics of applying for federal positions. Either way, you have come to the right place to gain more information about how to apply for federal positions.

You have a need and want for bettering your chances for obtaining either a new career or a change of career in the government sector.

Applying for federal government jobs can be complicated, difficult and scary to apply for if you have never done so before. In retrospect, government job applications are much like other job applications, with a few more steps in-between the application and job hiring stage of the candidate process.

There are some things that all potential government candidates must have to be successful, and the first step is to log on to USAJOBS.COM and create a user profile. The profile is fairly simple to fill out.

Once completed, there will be a section for uploading documents that will be "searchable" along with the profile, once the entire profile has been created changes to the profile may be changed at any given time. Just make sure to always "save" the profile or the changes will not be reflected in the profile.

As a side note: when completing a application in USAJOBS.GOV it is important to have your most recent information in the profile, the government agency will pull your user profile information and resume from your USAJOBS.GOV account. This is a major factor for all candidates using USAJOBS.GOV, since agencies have access to USAJOBS.GOV at all times.

It is a good practice to review resume and supplemental documents every time an application is applied for. This will give you an opportunity to ensure the information matches the position, which is being advertised.

This is a quick-step book for getting the basics for applying for government jobs. You will have other questions; on USAJOBS.GOV there is a "Frequently Asked Questions" section for candidates to review for free.

The FAQs section of USAJOBS.GOV is not only useful, but it further explains job announcements, eligibilities requirements and job processing time-lines to give a deeper aspect for what to expect on the job application has been submitted. It gives information about the responsibilities of the government agencies, the applicant and the hiring managers responsibilities as well.

This book will give additional clarity to the government hiring process and what you can do to make your experiences a bit easier, faster and more structured. The government hiring process can take up to 180 days, but there are things you as the job seeker, have access to during the duration of the entire hiring process. The key to your success in applying for government jobs or positions is organization, structure, patience and keeping motivated during the entire process.

You have come to the right place to start your journey toward your professional aspirations. Pay close attention, take notes and stay motivated.

All the Best,

Dr. Jenice Armstead

10 Tips for Applying to Government Jobs

The down turn of the United States economy affected everyone. A lack of jobs, employment opportunities and economy growth is around every corner of positivity.

No need to fret, there is hope for those whom want to earn employment with the federal government. Gaining employment in the federal sector hasn't always been an employment opportunity most would have considered in the past. But, with recent events many job seekers are finding refuge in the federal government.

There are plenty of advantages to working for the federal sector to include security and growth. Job seekers are looking for both of these aspects in an employment opportunity.

There is a way to obtain employment, gain job skills and grow oneself in this economy with looking at the federal sector as an open opportunity for success. Getting a job is hard enough as it is, why make the process any harder? That is what I am asked by candidates when they start to look at the government sector for employment. Some professional attributes toward obtaining a goal of getting a government position must include: persistence, determination, focus and constant drive for getting the desired job.

The amount of applications submitted to USAJOBS.GOV is countless. But, there is a way to "cut the fat" from the government application process for applicants.

The government job seeker must take on the same amount of responsibilities for their own career goals. Starting off with creating a excel spreadsheet, with keeping track of job announcements that have been submitted.

You must make sure to keep track of submissions and closing dates of the job announcements. Finally, conducting callbacks for those positions, which haven't sent a response for job announcement selection determination. As a taxpayer, the job seeker has a right to know where the federal agency stands with filling job announcement. Job candidates have a right to know if a job is closed for reasons of budget constraints or for a lack of qualified applicants. Either way, candidates have a right by law to know their status in the job hiring process when applying for federal positions. After all, it is your money that is funding the salaries of those whom are conduction the hiring for the federal government.

It is important to get feedback on the job announcement. This can be easily obtained by using email, by calling or writing a letter to get an update from the federal agency. This way, you are able to make notes on your status about the exact time period for a possible selection of a job announcement. This is why it is so important to be as organized as possible.

As I had been told many times while in the military, "if you don't keep track of your own records, nobody else will."

This means, you need to take responsibility for your own career, actions and life. It is important to outline your professional goals and your career aspirations. You are the only one who knows what you truly want, need and plan to succeed at with your life.

Let's take some time to see what you feel your goals are, this will help with identifying the professional clarity to ensure your focus is clear.

Start with writing down some professional goals and career aspirations, this can be changed or updated at any time.

My Professional Goal: _____

_____

_____

_____

_____

_____

My Career Aspirations: _____

_____

_____

_____

_____

_____

_____

Now that you have an idea of what your professional goals are and your career aspirations are with finding a government job, it is it is time to write down some positive affirmations to ensure you have somewhere to go when you start to doubt or feel dismayed about the government process.

Remember affirmations can be changed at any time to mirror any difficult situation. You can change your affirmations as your professional goals change, or as your career aspirations change.

Don't feel committed to any one affirmation; these are simply positive career tools to allow you to work toward your goals and aspirations. They can be long, short, statements, or visions of your professional future as you seek it to be.

Professional & Career Affirmations

I am professionally focused on progress

I am choosing to develop myself in my field

I am professionally admired in my field

I am moving in the direction best for me

I am able to work with anyone

I am skilled and talented in my profession

I am needed for my abilities and skills

I am outstanding in my field of _____

I am _____

I am _____

I am _____

I am _____

I am _____

I am _____

During any part of the federal job hiring process you can come back to your goals and affirmations to regain clarity about what the ultimate goal is. Let's begin the "10 Easy Tips for Apply for Government Jobs."

Enjoy,

Dr. Jenice Armstead

1) Open Your Mind

One of the best advantages of working for the federal government is having options. The job seeker is more versatile than ever before. There are variations of households; single parents and same-sex parents just to name a few. Your situation is unique toward your household. The key is to keep your mind wide open. An open mind attracts more opportunities than a closed mind. Take some quality time to think and research about the job opportunities with the federal government. The federal government has employment opportunities in a vast array of job descriptions. It is important to think and research the job descriptions and qualifications of the federal employment opportunities. There are plenty of locations and grade levels in the federal government to decide on. Accountants opportunities exist in virtually every federal agency, same for administration opportunities and information technology opportunities. It is false that all or most of federal positions only exist in Washington, D.C. Truth be told there are federal government employment opportunities all over the world. It is important to keep your mind open for opportunities, wherever they may be.

Open Minded Research Notes to Self

_____

_____

_____

_____

2) Getting Familiar and Friendly

This new economy requires more than any other economy in the United States history. Being familiar and friendly are keys for success. It is important to familiarize yourself with the federal government employment programs and how the programs function. An excellent source for gaining more information on the federal process is by going to www.usajobs.gov and reviewing the frequently asked questions section of the website. With reviewing these questions a better understanding of how jobs are structured and the processing time will clarify the federal process. These questions will break down how to know who is the point of contacts for federal positions and how to update resume information. This is where the

"Friendly" part comes in; as a federal position is funded by taxpayer's dollars the job seeker is free to contact the hiring manager or point of contact of the position to get more information on the federal position. Most job seekers are reprehensive about contacting the point of contact, but as the candidate you have right to get as much information about the position as possible. Ensuring you are friendly when you do get a person on the phone will benefit more than being aggressive.

Familiar & Friendly Notes to Self

_____

_____

_____

_____

_____

3) Know What To Look For

The federal job search is not an easy task; to many it can be down right intimidating and most never complete their first application. Federal applications have unfamiliar language and regulations related to them. There are two main elements to look for when applying for federal employment opportunities, and those are "Public" or "Merit" positions. Simply put, "Public" job announcements are those positions that any United States Citizen may apply for. Keeping in mind, the eligibility and qualification factors. "Merit" job announcements are those positions that current federal workers, prior federal workers, past federal workers, displaced federal workers, or United States Veterans may apply for. In the search, you may conduct an advance search for these key works to cut down on wasted time searching threw every federal position on the site. This is a critical element when searching for job announcements, at any given time a job seeker could spend a minimum of 8 to 10 hours a day searching through jobs without using this step to narrow down the job announcements they are eligible for. For instances, if you are looking for a Administrative Officer position, in Tampa, FL go to the "Advance Search" and type in "Administrative Officer, Tampa, FL, salary range, and public or merit." This will eliminate all the Administrative Officers that are not in your criteria and save you a ton of time and efforts that could be put toward a different search for more federal employment job opportunities.

4) Federal Job Announcements are Free

The main place to find any and all federal employment opportunities is www.usajobs.gov, which is a free site. In the mist of the down economy in the United States many scams and frauds have job seekers believing that they need to pay a employment agency a fee in order to apply for federal employment opportunities, this is a meth. All you have to do as a job seeker is log onto www.usajobs.gov, create a Profile, upload your resume and supplemental documents. This is all you need to start applying for federal employment job announcements. Although, USAJOBS is not an actual federal website, it is used for federal employment opportunities. You would still get the USAJOBS website if you did a search for www.usajob.com, this site takes you to the same FREE job announcement site for federal employment job opportunities.

Job Announcement Notes to Self

_____

_____

_____

_____

_____

_____

_____

5) Understand the Benefits of Federal Employment

Federal government employment opportunities are everywhere for all job positions; the benefits are just as extensive. Federal government job benefits include: Medical, dental, life insurance, long-term living assistance, retirement packages, tuition assistance reimbursement programs, relocation expenses paid, cost of living expenses paid, paid travel, paid certification & training time, on the job training, overtime, flextime job schedules, paid time off, annual vacations, and many other benefits. All federal government agencies don't necessarily have the same benefits packages. When conducting a search on USAJOBS, the agency will display a list of some benefits in the job announcement. If you click on the "tab" that states "benefits" you will see some of the possibilities of benefits to be including in the job announcements benefits packages. Keeping in mind, some benefits are not immediately effective for the potential new hire to utilize at the first day of employment. Some benefits have a time restriction, if it is important to you ask for more clarification on a particular benefit and the time restriction for the utilization of the benefit. In today's economy, an excellent benefit package can out weight a higher salary offer. Make sure to ask the questions needed to answer all information about benefits packages, you can also do some research on the federal agency website, or contact the human resources department to gain additional information.

6) Get Your Foot in the Door

The federal government has become a "career-builder" and any federal government job opportunity can be looked at as a "leg up" on the competition. The federal government sector, like many private sector businesses have started utilizing more internship programs as a means of "growing employees" into positions. Simply put, government internships are paid positions. They may be part-time or full-time positions depending on the program. The Student Temporary Employment Program (STEP) is a program to assist with helping current students gain work experience while still going to school. The benefit to the internship program is the flexible and opportunity to make additional income for the student. The agency keeps track of educational milestones of the employed student and graduation dates. In many cases the STEP Intern will be offered a position based on their time-in-position, generally an entry position with the possibility of growth for the future. Many executives received their "in" by utilizing internship programs such as the STEP program.

Another internship program is the Student Career Experience Program (SCEP) is a program focused on exposing the student to the career field, which the student is focused. Normally, an entry position this program allows for students to learn from their peers and supervisors in their educational field they are currently studying.

With both programs there are eligibly and qualification requirements for a potential candidate selection. Not all interns are offered a permanent position with the federal government agency, yet these programs are a method for potential permanent federal government employment and getting a "foot in the door."

Basic STEP/SCEP Eligibly Requirements

- ✓ Current Student
- ✓ Field of Choice
- ✓ Copies of Transcripts
- ✓ Agency Student Contract
- ✓ Part-Time or Full-Time

Job Seeker Notes

_____

_____

_____

_____

_____

_____

_____

_____

_____

_____

_____

_____

_____

_____

7) Being Ready at All Times

Federal government employment is all about always being ready, being the best and being the first. Federal employment opportunity is very competitive, it is important to have 3 resumes updated at all times. The 1st resume needs to show all the details of your career from current to last position. Keeping in mind all gaps in employment need to be justified and explained. The federal government employment process is all about explain every single position held. The 2nd resume needs to be a bit shorter than the 1st, the last resume needs to be a 1 page – quick read resume. Only include the mandatory items: Name, address, email, phone number, jobs held and education. When going to federal government job interviews always have extra resumes, extra references, and copies of your education transcripts, certifications, training information and samples of your work. Even if it isn't mentioned, offer the material at the end of the interview.

Items to Keep with You At All Times

Updated Resumes

Update References

Copies of Education

Copies of Training

Other Documents

_____

_____

_____

_____

8) Keep the Patience of "Job"

Job was a Biblical historical character who overcame every obstacle in his life by having great faith. Job had the faith of a mustard seed and unwavering faith. When going through the federal government hiring process it is important to keep your patience through the entire process. The federal government hiring process time ranges from 30 – 180 days (1 months – 6 months) from submitting the job application to being hired. Many times candidates get frustrated with the entire process, feel stagnate and start to doubt their qualifications for positions. The federal sector has more candidates than ever before, the competition is thick, but the reward is well worth the wait. If there is a point of contact on the job announcement, call to seek the status of the hiring manager. Keep a list of email point of contacts for the agency and email the contacts to obtain a current status of the position. Keep a list of affirmations to read outlook to yourself, this builds a positive outlook on your job search. All in all, keep your patience and stay positive in your job seeking experience.

Patience Affirmation Reminders

I will find the career of my dreams

I am working on the right path for my success

I am a willing participate in my own success

I have what it takes to find my career

I have the right qualifications for the job

I am the best candidate for the position

I am working toward success

9) Keep Calm and Search On

The federal government employment process is a lengthy process; policy and procedures of the federal government employment process can be down right grueling. The key to the wait is to keep calm and search on with your job opportunities for other federal employment. As I always say, "Don't put all of your job applications in on email box." The great part about USAJOBS is the variety it gives the job seeker. All jobs have different needs in the federal government sector, yet you can find plenty of variety in even the most common job. For instance, Administrative Officer duties will vary from Department of Defense to Department of Agriculture. While the wait happens, why now search for other positions that may be of interest. Give yourself plenty of opportunity; the wait could be longer or shorter from job announcement to job announcement. Keep calm and continue on with more searches, what could it hurt? Job seekers need to keep themselves open to all possible job opportunities.

Calming Affirmations for Success

I am calm and collective about my job search

I am calm and aware of possible outcomes

I am calm and assured about my opportunities

I am calm and knowledgably about my field

I am calm and aware of my success

I am calm and aware of my professional worth

I am calm and assured of my future

I am calm and aware of everything working out

10) Take All Options as Opportunities

The common job seeker has come from: I want a job to I need a job. Have you ever realized the options of opportunities that are right before your eyes? Federal government employment opportunities are everywhere. Federal government, state and local government all have job employment openings almost on a monthly, weekly or daily basis. Don't feel afraid to check USAJOBS on a daily basis. The job seeker may also set up "Saved Searches," which are common searches that are saved in the profile section, in order to save time with job announcement searches. Job announcements that match the "Saved Search" are directly emailed to accounts connected to USAJOBS.

This is an option with even more opportunity. The reason why it is important to set up "Saved Searches" is when applying for job announcements in the federal government, it matters who submits their application first. That's right! The federal government employment process is all about "Weights and Scores." Simply put, applicant's complete questions that have a "weight and score" to each question. Depending on how well the applicant answers, and the time the application is submitted, depends on whether or not the application will be among the top percent to receive consideration for review. The key is to complete the application in its entirety, as quickly as possible, and submit the application before other applicants before the deadline.

Conclusion

The job seekers have many opportunities to take advantage of by applying for federal sector job announcements. There are many benefits to working for the federal government. The federal process is lengthy, but the hiring procedures have been revamped and improved during this last Presidential Administration. The keys to applying for federal sector positions are completing the profile and uploading of a resume, being organizational and conducting status updates on applications, which have been applied for. Positive affirmations help with keeping the job seeker focused and motivated. The federal sector is full of job opportunities, whether it full-time, part-time, internships, or volunteer opportunities. The federal sector is hiring and the locations are unlimited. Now the job seeker has tips for how to apply for federal sector jobs with ease. Happy federal job hunting! Stay motivated and focused, remember you can do anything you put your mind to.

All the Best to You,

Dr. Jenice Armstead

Photo Credit: Robert Cass

Government Job Announcement Notes

Job Announcement #_____

Job Title_____

Date Applied_____

Date Announcement Closed_____

Job Location_____

Salary Range_____

Grade Level_____

Point of Contact Info_____

Interview Date_____

Job Announcement #_____

Job Title_____

Date Applied_____

Date Announcement Closed_____

Job Location_____

Salary Range_____

Grade Level_____

Point of Contact Info_____

Interview Date_____

Job Announcement #_____

Job Title_____

Date Applied_____

Date Announcement Closed_____

Job Location_____

Salary Range_____

Grade Level_____

Point of Contact Info_____

Interview Date_____

Job Announcement #_____

Job Title_____

Date Applied_____

Date Announcement Closed_____

Job Location_____

Salary Range_____

Grade Level_____

Point of Contact Info_____

Interview Date_____

Job Announcement #_____

Job Title_____

Date Applied_____

Date Announcement Closed_____

Job Location_____

Salary Range_____

Grade Level_____

Point of Contact Info_____

Interview Date_____

Job Announcement #_____

Job Title_____

Date Applied_____

Date Announcement Closed_____

Job Location_____

Salary Range_____

Grade Level_____

Point of Contact Info_____

Interview Date_____

Job Announcement #_____

Job Title_____

Date Applied_____

Date Announcement Closed_____

Job Location_____

Salary Range_____

Grade Level_____

Point of Contact Info_____

Interview Date_____

Job Announcement #_____

Job Title_____

Date Applied_____

Date Announcement Closed_____

Job Location_____

Salary Range_____

Grade Level_____

Point of Contact Info_____

Interview Date_____

Job Announcement #_____

Job Title_____

Date Applied_____

Date Announcement Closed_____

Job Location_____

Salary Range_____

Grade Level_____

Point of Contact Info_____

Interview Date_____

Job Announcement #_____

Job Title_____

Date Applied_____

Date Announcement Closed_____

Job Location_____

Salary Range_____

Grade Level_____

Point of Contact Info_____

Interview Date_____

Job Announcement #_____

Job Title_____

Date Applied_____

Date Announcement Closed_____

Job Location_____

Salary Range_____

Grade Level_____

Point of Contact Info_____

Interview Date_____

Job Announcement #_____

Job Title_____

Date Applied_____

Date Announcement Closed_____

Job Location_____

Salary Range_____

Grade Level_____

Point of Contact Info_____

Interview Date_____

Job Announcement #_____

Job Title_____

Date Applied_____

Date Announcement Closed_____

Job Location_____

Salary Range_____

Grade Level_____

Point of Contact Info_____

Interview Date_____

Job Announcement #_____

Job Title_____

Date Applied_____

Date Announcement Closed_____

Job Location_____

Salary Range_____

Grade Level_____

Point of Contact Info_____

Interview Date_____

Job Announcement #_____

Job Title_____

Date Applied_____

Date Announcement Closed_____

Job Location_____

Salary Range_____

Grade Level_____

Point of Contact Info_____

Interview Date_____

Job Announcement #_____

Job Title_____

Date Applied_____

Date Announcement Closed_____

Job Location_____

Salary Range_____

Grade Level_____

Point of Contact Info_____

Interview Date_____

Job Announcement #_____

Job Title_____

Date Applied_____

Date Announcement Closed_____

Job Location_____

Salary Range_____

Grade Level_____

Point of Contact Info_____

Interview Date_____

Job Announcement #_____

Job Title_____

Date Applied_____

Date Announcement Closed_____

Job Location_____

Salary Range_____

Grade Level_____

Point of Contact Info_____

Interview Date_____

Job Announcement #_____

Job Title_____

Date Applied_____

Date Announcement Closed_____

Job Location_____

Salary Range_____

Grade Level_____

Point of Contact Info_____

Interview Date_____

Job Announcement #_____

Job Title_____

Date Applied_____

Date Announcement Closed_____

Job Location_____

Salary Range_____

Grade Level_____

Point of Contact Info_____

Interview Date_____

Job Announcement #_____

Job Title_____

Date Applied_____

Date Announcement Closed_____

Job Location_____

Salary Range_____

Grade Level_____

Point of Contact Info_____

Interview Date_____

Job Announcement #_____

Job Title_____

Date Applied_____

Date Announcement Closed_____

Job Location_____

Salary Range_____

Grade Level_____

Point of Contact Info_____

Interview Date_____

Job Announcement #_____

Job Title_____

Date Applied_____

Date Announcement Closed_____

Job Location_____

Salary Range_____

Grade Level_____

Point of Contact Info_____

Interview Date_____

Job Announcement #_____

Job Title_____

Date Applied_____

Date Announcement Closed_____

Job Location_____

Salary Range_____

Grade Level_____

Point of Contact Info_____

Interview Date_____

References

Armstead, J. (n.d.). Jenice Armstead. *Welcome To Jenice Armstead*. Retrieved January 3, 2013, from http://www.jenicearmstead.com

Frequently Asked Questions. (n.d.). *USAJOBS*. Retrieved January 2, 2013, from www.usajobs.gov

Jenice Armstead's Contributor Profile - Yahoo! Contributor Network - contributor.yahoo.com. (n.d.). *Contributor*. Retrieved January 3, 2013, from http://contributor.yahoo.com/user/793 794/jenice_armstead.html

Students & Recent Graduates. (n.d.).

www.opm.gov. Retrieved January 3, 2013,

from http://beta.opm.gov/policy-data-

oversight/hiring-authorities/students-

recent-graduates/

www.ingramcontent.com/pod-product-compliance
Lightning Source LLC
Chambersburg PA
CBHW021901170526
45157CB00005B/1913